SPENDING TIME WITH GOD

God's Daily Presence Fulfills Your Greatest Purpose

James Thomas

Copyright © 2014 by **James Thomas**

All rights reserved. No part of this publication may be reproduced, distributed or transmitted in any form or by any means, without prior written permission.

Sermon To Book
www.sermontobook.com

Spending Time With God / James Thomas
ISBN-13: 9780692324189
ISBN-10: 0692324186

I dedicate this book to my lovely wife Tonya who has been my biggest supporter in life. To my Pastor, Dr. Denny D. Davis, Senior Pastor of The St. John Church Unleashed of Grand Prairie Texas, for encouraging me to live up to my potential. To my friend and mentor, Jeffrey A. Johnson, Senior Pastor of The Eastern Star Church of Indianapolis Indiana, for inspiring me to write this book for circulation. And to the members of The Rhema Life Fellowship Church of whom I have the distinct privilege to be the Senior Pastor and Founder. You are beautiful people.

CONTENTS

4 Disciplines That Motivate & Inspire STWG 1
Required Elements For Spending Time With God 7
The Impact Of Spending Quality Time With God 13
The Power Of Prayer.. 17
Stay In The Closet.. 27
Read Your Bible... 33
Your Praise Is Your Weapon 39
Good Works 45
The Consequences Of Not Spending Time With God 67
Here I Am To Worship 71
Share Jesus Now 87
About The Author 90
About SermonToBook.Com 92

INTRODUCTION

4 Disciplines That Motivate & Inspire STWG

In this book, I will address the importance of spending time with God by concentrating on four disciplines which will motivate and inspire you to examine how much time you are currently spending with God, and to challenge you to make the decision to deliberately start spending quality time with Him.

The 4 disciplines include:

1. **Fasting and praying**
2. **Time in His Word**
3. **Praise and worship**
4. **Good works**

All four of these disciplines are essential to spending quality time with God, and fulfilling our created purpose in life. When I taught these same principles to the members of our Church in Plano, Texas, we saw the power and grace of God move like never before in our congregation and in the community. This book is designed to help individuals develop a personal, daily discipline of spending time with God.

Our Greatest Privilege

Spending time with God is one of the greatest privileges you have in life. Greater than your public worship, greater than your spiritual gifts, greater than preaching and teaching the gospel. When you commit yourself to spending time with your Heavenly Father on a daily basis, it will change your life. In fact, the number one call for a disciple of Jesus Christ is to be with Him, to follow Him, to spend time with Him.

Consider Mark 3:13-15: "And he went up on the mountain and called to himself those he himself wanted, and they came to him. Then he appointed twelve, that they might be with him, and that he might send them out to preach. And to have power to heal sickness and to cast out demons."

God wants to spend time with us, not because He's lonely or needs our company, but because we so desperately need His daily presence in order to fulfill our greatest purpose, which is to please Him.

The 3 Primary Reasons For Spending Time With God

1) *God Created You in His Image and for His Pleasure*

We were made with the capacity to commune with our Creator. Genesis 1:25-27 says: "When God created the animals, he created them after their own kind, but when he created man, he created them in his own image, after his own likeness" (NKJ).

As human beings, we possess the blessed gift to interact with God. We are reminded in Colossians 1:16 that, "All things were made by and for his pleasure" (NKJ). Therefore, as His creation, it is our duty and responsibility to spend time with our Creator.

2) You Can't Bear Fruit without STWG (Spending Time with God)

You will never grow more like Christ if you neglect to spend time with Him. Jesus says, "I am the vine, and you are the branches, he who abides in me and I in him bears much fruit, for without me you can do nothing" (John 15:5, NKJ).

Aren't you tired of having the same unhealthy spiritual life you've had for the past few years? I was, and it wasn't until I decided to engage in a daily devotion with my Lord that I began bearing fruit in my life. It is our Spiritual Intake that determines our Spiritual Growth. Our full potential as followers of Jesus Christ can only be obtained through a vibrant relationship with God. Matthew 4:4 says: "Man shall not live by bread alone, but by every word that proceeds out of the mouth of God" (NKJ).

3) *STWG Allows You to Get to Know Him*

How can you expect to know someone on an intimate level unless you spend time with them? It's difficult to love people you barely know; it's unnatural to trust people you don't know; and it's nearly impossible to obey people you don't trust. The same is true with your relationship with God. If you intentionally spend time with Him, with the purpose of getting to know Him better, you will be motivated to love Him, obey Him, and trust Him with your entire life. You will shatter the chains of your imprisonments, become stronger in every aspect of your life, and experience the peace that only comes through knowing Him.

As with every discipline, sacrifices must be made in order to accomplish the end goal. There are certain barriers and hindrances we must overcome on our journey to spending quality time with God. Let me assure you that making sacrifices is the key component over making excuses. When it comes to spending time with God, there are many explanations, reasons, and excuses for why we fail to obligate ourselves to the greatest privilege we have.

Common Excuses We Make to Avoid Time with God

I'm Too Busy

When you are prompted to spend time with God, you might think: "I am just too busy. I have to work; I have to pay bills; I have to take care of my family; I have to go to school; my schedule is too crowded; I have too much on my plate."

Don't get me wrong, all of these things are important, but you must learn to prioritize your life in order to create a sense of balance. God has given each of us the same 24 hours in a day, and we usually make time for what is important to us. My wife, Tonya, helped me see this reality in our own marriage. She recently asked me, "Why don't we spend time together like we used to?" I responded with a list of excuses, concluding with, "I just don't have the time!" She said, "The reason you don't *have* the time is because you don't *make* the time." Where does spending time with God rank on your priority list each day?

I'm In Bondage

Some believers genuinely desire daily time with God, but they're trapped in the bondage of a particular sin or bad habit. And every time they decide to open their Bible, they find themselves pulled by the force of their old nature and perverted passions.

Your complete emancipation from bondage rests in the presence of the Lord! You *can* break away from every sin by exposing yourself to the presence of the Spirit of God. "Where the Spirit of the Lord is, there is liberty" (2 Corinthians 3:17, NKJ).

I Don't Understand The Benefits

You might think, "I've been reading my Bible for years, but I don't really see the benefit of it in my life. Why continue? What's the point?" Even if you can't comprehend the advantages of spending time with God, you can be fully assured that it's extremely beneficial to every aspect of your life, (i.e. your marriage, your family, your church, your ministry, your job, your finances, your self-esteem, and so much more). The reality is, there are so many benefits to spending time with God that this book could never begin to capture its entirety.

Are you ready, by the grace of our amazing Savior, to start *Spending Time With God*?

CHAPTER ONE

Required Elements For Spending Time With God

In order to spend time with God, you must have a sincere desire. This desire is not something you can simply conjure up. You must pray that God would renew your vision and passion to be in His presence on a daily basis. Once you possess that desire, here are some practical steps to enhance your time with God.

Set A Specific Time

Whether you spend time with God in the morning, afternoon or evening, you must choose a time that works best for you. It's important to set a time when you're alert, energized, and mentally prepared. The Psalmist seemed to prefer mornings (Psalm 5:3), but whatever time you choose, make sure you are consistent. Make a habit to open your Bible at the same time each day, anticipating your scheduled time with the Lord, and refuse to allow anything or anyone to prevent you from meeting

God on time. Whether you spend 5 minutes or 15 minutes, honor God by being consistent with your time.

Choose A Special Place

Whether it's in your car, office, closet, or couch, you need to identify a place where you can spend time with God—a place unheard by man, unseen by man, and free of distractions. Luke 22:39 says, "When Jesus prepared to spend time with the Father, he went to the Mount of Olives, as he usually did." That was His place to commune with His father. You need a place too, other than Sunday morning during the public worship service. Start examining potential locations where you can set aside time to connect with God in private.

Ask yourself: Where can or do I spend quality time with God? _____.

Gather The Necessary Resources

When I prepare to spend time with God, I collect all the materials I may need before I begin. That way, I can be fully present in the moment without having to get up and grab something I forgot. Consider bringing your computer or some other device to take notes. For prayer, bring a floor mat for kneeling. Start a prayer journal to record your prayer requests. Bring a prayer shawl. If you'd like to incorporate worship into your time, bring a songbook or a CD player and play worshipful music. These are all simply suggestions to get you thinking.

Remember, your time with God will be as impactful as you make it.

Follow A Simple Plan

Do not complicate this glorious privilege. The ultimate purpose of spending time with God is not to become a theologian or a walking biblical dictionary, but to learn to enjoy basking in the presence of the Almighty. Keep it simple! Now that you have selected a specific time and place to meet with God, and you've gathered all the necessary resources, here is a simple, yet effective, plan to spend 10-15 minutes each day with God.

Relax

Be still and get quiet. Take a few deep breaths and start preparing your heart for the moment. As simple as it may sound, some people struggle with relaxing because they are always thinking about other things and other people. For the next few moments, just allow yourself to block out everything and everyone, so that you can calm yourself to spend time with God.

Read

Open your Bible to a portion of Scripture, maybe even a verse or an entire chapter and read it. You may not understand certain words or phrases, but just reading the Word will bless your experience. The book of Proverbs is a good book to read because it has 31 chapters to correspond with 31 days in a month. Perhaps you can read one chapter each day. Don't rush through the Scriptures. Take time to read the Infallible Word of the Living God.

Reflect

Reflect on the passage you've just read. What does it mean to you? How does it specifically apply to your life? What does God mean to you? How does His goodness impact your life? Think about His holiness, His righteousness, His standards, His attributes.

Record

Write down your thoughts, feelings and contemplations of what you just read. What do you believe God is saying specifically to you through His Word? Is there a promise to claim? Is there a person to forgive in your life? Is there a principle to practice? Is there a vision to pursue? If so, write it down!

Reverence

Acknowledge the presence of God. He is with you in spirit and in truth, so from your heart ascribe all the worth that you can unto God. This is a great opportunity to worship Him by standing, kneeling or sitting. Lift up your hands and open your mouth in songs and expressions of gratitude and reverence. Thank Him for everything that you can think of verbally. Give Him glory!

Requests

Now is the time to petition God through your prayers. It is no coincidence that this step is listed last. Most of the time when we approach God, our requests are at the top of the list, or in many cases the only thing on the list at all. What I have discovered in the process of spending time with God is that He is already completely aware of all my needs, and sometimes He will meet them even when I fail or forget to ask. Too often we are more concerned with getting our needs met than we are with spending time with God. As a result, we only approach Him in order to get our needs met. Getting your needs met is not the purpose of meeting with God, but whenever you approach Him to delight in His presence, He will in fact meet you at your point of need. Whatever you ask, ask in faith, believing that your God is willing and able to perform it.

You will not believe the impact this will have on your life.

CHAPTER TWO

The Impact Of Spending Quality Time With God

What happens when you spend time with God on a daily basis? Will your face shine like Moses? What are the results? Spending quality time with God will impact your life in 6 ways:

1) STWG Gets Your Attention On God

Sometimes we can become distracted by the cares of this world. As a consequence, we lose focus of our relationship with God. Whatever we give our attention to, we inevitably begin to worship and emulate. We eventually become what we intently behold, because we are automatically drawn to what we are fixated upon. By spending quality time with God, we can adjust our focus so that we become more like our God in character, in nature, and in priority.

Have you lost your focus in life? You can rediscover it by basking in the presence of God.

2) STWG Helps Us Get Our Directions From God

Time spent in God's presence will reveal His will for your life. You will gain instruction and guidance from the Lord. My son Jordan would never completely understand my expectations and plans for his life by remaining disconnected from his fellowship with me. There are so many questions about life that can only be answered by your Heavenly Father.

People often ask me, "Pastor, what is God's will for my life?" God alone can answer that question with absolute certainty! When you are in His presence, you are in the place of revelations. Let God lead you beside still waters and into green pastures. While in His presence, commit your day to Him.

3) STWG Helps Us Grow To Become Like Jesus

Is your ultimate goal to become more and more like Jesus? Spending time with Him gives you a great opportunity to learn how. The more time you spend with God, the more you can grow and become like Him. Assimilation by association means taking on the certain characteristics of your associations. Very few things in life will cause spiritual growth like STWG. Make a decision to grow closer to Christ today. Break away from the monotonous spiritual rut you're in. Position yourself face-to-face with the Spirit of God. Get started right now!

4) STWG Increases Joy In Your Life

Psalm 16:11 says, "In his presence there is fullness of joy." When you are in the presence of God, all worries, stresses, and anxieties are replaced with the joy of the Lord. You don't have to be depressed another day. You can go before your Father in Heaven and release all your concerns to Him. Instead of allowing your circumstances to determine your happiness, experience the real joy found in the presence of God.

5) STWG Gives Us Calming Peace

In John 20:19, 21, and 26, Jesus appears to the disciples and says, "Peace be unto you." Wherever Jesus is, there is peace in high definition, a peace that surpasses all understanding, a peace that will strengthen you in times of adversity, a peace that will calm you in the midst of a storm. Mr. Horatio Spafford penned the following lyrics after his three young daughters died in a shipwreck crossing the Atlantic Ocean. Instead of complaining to God about his loss, he simply went before God and experienced a calming, God-given peace as he penned the words:

"When peace like a river attendeth my way, when sorrows like sea billows roll, whatever my lot thou hast taught me to say, it is well with my soul."

6) By STWG You Will Experience The Favor Of God

God is pleased when His creation spends time with Him, and whenever God is pleased, favor ensues. When the favor of God is on your life, blessings manifest often and miraculously. Doors will open and things will begin to work in your favor. But please note: Favor is a by-product of spending time with God, not the purpose. Favor simply comes with the territory. Spending time with God attracts His best for your life. One moment in the presence of God can set the wheels of blessings in motion for you and your entire family.

This is the power of spending time with God.

CHAPTER THREE

The Power Of Prayer

Be anxious for nothing, but in everything by prayer and supplication, with thanksgiving, let your requests be made known to God. — Philippians 4:6

If you struggle with stress or anxiety, listen closely.

- 40% of the things we worry about never happen.

- 30% of the things we worry about have already happened in the past and we can't change.

- 12% of the things we worry about are what we think others are thinking about us.

- 10% of what we worry about is petty, insignificant and unimportant to life.

- Only 8% of our worry is legitimate concern.

- Nearly 40 million Americans struggle with some type of stress or anxiety disorder.

- There have been more books written about coping with worry/stress/anxiety than any other subject.

- There have been more medicine and drugs prescribed to cope with worry/stress/anxiety than any other prescription.

There is an African proverb that says, "The only type of worry that is good is when you worry about the fact that you worry too much. Worms eat you when you are dead, but worry eats you when you are alive."

There is a distinct difference between "concern" and "worry." It is human nature to be concerned about some things, but if we are not careful, Satan will cause those concerns to turn into worry. Worry is a mental state of restlessness and agitation brought on by fear and/or doubt, because worry always anticipates the worst. When we worry as children of God, we are literally tormenting ourselves by taking the pain out of yesterday and the pain out of tomorrow and bringing it into today. It is a sin for you to be consumed by worry.

Here are 4 reasons not to worry as a Christian:

1) Worry Accomplishes Absolutely Nothing

Worrying is a waste of time and energy. It will not solve any problems or bring resolution to any situation.

It is a fruitless activity. When we worry, it is an indicator that we really don't trust God. Jesus said in Matthew 6:27, "Which of you by worrying can add a single hour to his life?" Worrying is unproductive; it leads nowhere; and it paralyzes rather than energizes.

2) Worry Is Not Good For You

Worry is destructive in so many ways, (i.e. physically, emotionally, psychologically, mentally, spiritually, etc.). This leads to ulcers, high blood pressure, heart problems, headaches, colon distress, and so much more. The suicide rate is at an all-time high because worry causes you to believe that either God is not capable or that God doesn't care, and neither one is true. "Worry weighs down the heart" (Proverbs 12:25). Another translation says, "Worry wears down the heart."

3) Worry Is The Opposite Of Trusting God

When you worry, you're basically saying, "God, I don't trust you." That's why Jesus condemns worry, because it shows a lack of confidence in the person, the character, and the ability of our God. The time and energy we spend worrying would be better spent in prayer and trusting God. Matthew 6:25-26 says, "Therefore I tell you, do not worry about your life, what you shall eat or drink; or about your body, what you shall wear. Is not life more important than food, and the body more important than clothes? Look at the birds of the air, they do not sow or reap or store away in barns, and yet your heavenly father feeds them. Are you not much more valuable than they are? Oh ye of little faith."

4) Worry Puts Your Focus In The Wrong Direction

When you worry, your perspective gets skewed. You begin to focus on things that are secondary. In the process, you lose sight of what is really important and primary in life. Matthew 6:33 says, "Seek ye first the Kingdom of God, and all these things shall be added unto thee." The kingdom is primary; our provisions are secondary. Any time our provisions become primary, then the things of God become secondary. As long as we put God first, He will add to our lives, but when He is secondary, we worry about adding to our lives.

The Ultimate Antidote For Worry

In one single verse, the Apostle Paul gives us the cure for worry. Philippians 4:6 says, "Be anxious for nothing, but in everything by prayer and supplication with thanksgiving let your requests be made known to God," (Philippians 4:6).

There is no problem, no circumstance, and no situation that cannot be brought before our Heavenly Father in prayer. You don't have to hide in the shadow of your mistakes, or withhold your most humiliating realities. You can tell God anything. Unlike man, you don't have to worry about God spreading your business around. The moment you tell God your struggles is not the moment you are informing Him of them. He already knows what you're going through. When you pray, you invite His involvement.

The 'Immovable' Rock

A little boy was spending Saturday morning playing in his sandbox. In the process of creating roads and tunnels for his toy cars, he discovered a large rock in the middle of the sandbox. The boy dug around the rock, managing to dislodge it from the dirt. Using his feet, he nudged the rock across the sandbox.

He was a small boy and this was a large rock. When he got it to the edge of the sandbox, he couldn't roll it over the wall of the sandbox. Determined, the little boy pushed with all his might, but every time he thought he'd succeeded, the rock fell back into the sandbox. In the process, he smashed his fingers and burst into tears of frustration.

All this time the boy's father watched the scene unfold from the living room window. The moment the tear fell, a large shadow fell across the boy and the sandbox. It was the boy's father. Gently, but firmly he said, "Son, why didn't you use all the strength you had available?" Defeated, the boy sobbed back, "But I did, daddy, I did. I used all the strength I had!"

The father kindly corrected his son. "No," he said, "you didn't use all the strength you had. You didn't ask me." The father reached down, picked up the rock, and removed it from the sandbox.

What a friend we have in Jesus!

Be Specific When You Pray

"Be anxious for nothing, but in everything by prayer and *supplication* with thanksgiving let your requests be made known to God" (Philippians 4:6).

To supplicate means to humbly petition God by specifying your exact need. Whatever is worrying you, learn to take it to God and be specific about it. Supplication is not being selfish in your prayers, but being aware of what you need God to do in your life. Supplication is the most intense form of prayer because it conveys a sense of urgency in the request. There is nothing wrong with asking God to bless your family, heal your coworker, save your spouse, or heal a friend, but don't forget to pray for yourself.

Remember, flight attendants always encourage you to put on your oxygen mask first before assisting others.

Find Something To Be Thankful For

"Be anxious for nothing, but in everything by prayer and supplication *with thanksgiving* let your requests be made known to God" (Philippians 4:6).

Paul warns against fretting, but instead encourages us to express our gratitude to God in every situation. It doesn't matter how bad your circumstances appear, you can always find something to thank God for. So often we take the blessings He gives us for granted, and thus, miss out on opportunities to give Him praise.

Consider William Devaughn's words:

Though you may not drive a great big Cadillac
Diamond in the back, sunroof top
Diggin' the scene
With a gangsta lean
Gangsta whitewalls
TV antennas in the back

You may not have a car at all
But remember brothers and sisters
You can still stand tall
Just be thankful for what you've got

7 Hindrances To Prayer

1. *Unrepentant Sin in Your Life*

"If I regard iniquity in my heart, the Lord will not hear me" (Psalm 66:18).

2. *Strained relationships with your spouse*

"Likewise, ye husbands, dwell with them according to knowledge, giving honor unto the wife, as unto the weaker vessel, and as being heirs together of the grace of life; that your prayers be not hindered" (1 Peter 3:7).

3. *Unreconciled wrongs, debts, or offenses between Christian brothers and sisters*

"Therefore if you bring your gift to the altar, and there remember that your brother has something against you, leave your gift there before the altar, and go your way. First be reconciled to your brother, and then come and offer your gift" (Matthew 5:23–24).

4. An Unforgiving or Bitter Spirit

"Then Peter came and said to Him, 'Lord, how often shall my brother sin against me and I forgive him? Up to seven times?' Jesus said to him, 'I do not say to you, up to seven times, but up to seventy times seven'" (Matthew 18:21–22).

"And be ye kind one to another, tenderhearted, forgiving one another, even as God for Christ's sake hath forgiven you" (Ephesians 4:32).

5. Covetousness

"From whence come wars and fighting's among you? Come they not hence, even of your lusts that war in your members? Ye lust, and have not: ye kill, and desire to have, and cannot obtain: ye fight and war, yet ye have not, because ye ask not. Ye ask, and receive not, because ye ask amiss, that ye may consume it upon your lusts" (James 4:1–3).

6. Neglecting the Word of God

"He that turneth away his ear from hearing the law, even his prayer shall be abomination" (Proverbs 28:9).

7. *Prayerlessness*

"Moreover as for me, God forbid that I should sin against the Lord in ceasing to pray for you: but I will teach you the good and the right way" (1 Samuel 12:23).

CHAPTER FOUR

Stay In The Closet

Let me ease any apprehensions you may have concerning the chapter title. I am simply talking about the power of personal prayer with God. I believe the missing ingredient in church today is lack of prayer. We don't pray like we used to pray. The church of old used to meet and pray until God manifested His presence. Nobody was watching the clock on the wall. They used to tarry in the spirit until God moved, no matter how long it took. As a result of our passive approach to prayer, there are churches packed with people, but they lack real power for the supernatural.

We have bigger bodies, buildings, and budgets but have fewer breakthroughs in the body of Christ. The reason why we don't see miracles and deliverance today is not because God has lost His power, but because we have lost our power due to our refusal to pray. If the church of Jesus Christ could get back to the privilege and priority of prayer, our children would grow up, prisons would close up, families would build up, drug trade would dry up, and our critics would have to shut up.

The strongest force in the universe is not the composition of nuclear energy, nor the might of human strength. The strongest force is the church on their hands and knees in prayer. When the church prays, things happen. Remember the account in Acts. When Peter was chained to a legion of guards in prison, the church began praying. As they prayed, God dispatched an angel and set Peter free. Before the people had finished praying, Peter was knocking on their door. Private prayer is profitable for your pilgrimage on this planet!

Overcome Temptation

Remember Matthew 4. When Satan tried to tempt Jesus with food, fame, and a form of religion, Jesus was able to overcome each temptation. Why? Because He had just come out of the wilderness where He had fasted 40 days. That's why the saints of old used to say, "Stay prayed-up, because you never know what the devil is going to bring your way."

Many of our daily struggles could be eliminated if we took our requests to the altar of prayer. You don't have to fall for every trick of the enemy. You don't have to be enticed with every perversion. You can live a life of liberty and victory if you get your prayer life right.

Focus On The Spoken Word

Sometimes you have to go off by yourself to get the revelation you need from the Word of God. It's hard to hear God when you are surrounded by the chaos of so many other voices. You might be spiritually confused because you are believing every prophecy that comes your way. Take a moment and close your ears to those around you and open your heart in prayer to God's Word.

Each time Satan tempts Jesus in Luke, Jesus says, "It is written." Sometimes when I read the Bible I run across things I can't quite comprehend. Commentaries and colleagues will offer their interpretation, but then my understanding is subjected to another's ideology. Sometimes the only way to begin to understand what God is saying is through intense fasting and praying. Prayer is more than you talking to God. It gives God an opportunity to talk to you.

Fellowship Without Distractions

You are never going to truly enjoy God publicly until you can enjoy Him privately in prayer. When I'm in my prayer closet, I don't have to worry about who's looking at me, what I'm wearing, who likes me, and so on. God gets all of my attention, and He gives me all the attention I need. I don't have to be concerned with the pressure of trying to please others. Whether I want to sit and weep, kneel down, prostrate myself, or jump up and down, I don't have to worry about anyone judging me. Because in my closet, it's just me and God!

Praying For The Audience Of One

When Neil Anderson was a child, they never asked him to say grace at school, because whenever Neil said grace, he always said grace for the entire cafeteria. One time when he was praying privately, his friend leaned over and said, "I can't hear you." Neil said, "That's all right, because I wasn't talking to you!"

Cultivating The Proper Motive

In Matthew 6, Jesus is on the side of a mountain preaching to his followers about the importance of having proper motives. Whether it's giving to the needy or praying, Jesus is more concerned with our motive than the act itself. If somebody has to blow a trumpet or announce your offering every time you give, you are giving with the wrong motivation. Matthew 6:3 says, "But when you give to the needy, don't let your left hand know what your right hand is doing."

Give with a low profile. Be discreet. There is only one proper motive for giving and that is to help those in need.

The Priority For Private Prayer

Matthew 6:5 says, "Don't be like the hypocrites, for they love to pray standing in the synagogue, and in the corners of streets, that they may be seen of men." Their prayers may be public, but they are essentially pretentious. It's nothing more than a pious act to be seen by the eyes of man. The only reward they qualify for is the reward of knowing somebody saw and heard them pray.

Learn to meet God in private. Matthew 6:6 says, "When you pray, enter into your closet, and when you have closed the door, pray to the father." This is not a prohibition to public prayer. God is not against us praying in public, but He wants us to guard our prayer lives against self-satisfying and self-observed prayers.

Now, let's talk about prayer's perfect companion: reading your Bible.

CHAPTER FIVE

Read Your Bible

What makes the Bible different from any other book? It is God's book. He gave it to us to tell us about Himself (2 Peter 1:21). And because the Bible is about God and His salvation, it is also about the Son of God, our Savior. There are so many wonderful blessings that will come when you take time to read the Bible.

The Bible is the most important book in the world for many reasons. When we read and listen to Scripture, there are many benefits to our faith in God, but we must never substitute knowledge for obedience to God. Living by the Word of God is what causes us to possess His promises for our lives.

9 reasons to read your Bible

1. To know God better.

2. To grow in your spiritual life.

3. To understand God's will for your life.

4. To perpetuate the Christian legacy.

5. To strengthen your witness for Jesus Christ.

6. To expose false doctrine and teaching.

7. To recognize the presence of your sin.

8. To receive guidance for your daily life.

9. To obey God.

Read your Bible Inquisitively

As you read your Bible, ask yourself these questions:

- Is there any command to obey?

- Is there any promise to believe?

- Is there a good example to follow?

- Is there a sin to avoid?

- Do I learn anything about God?

- Do I learn anything about man?

- Is there anything I can thank God for?

5 Reasons to Live by the Word of God

1. It is our duty as sons and daughters of God (Acts 20:28).

2. God's commands are for our own good (Ephesians 2:10).

3. To reap future blessing (1 Corinthians 15:14-18).

4. To share God's love with others (John 14:15).

5. To serve as a credible witness to the gospel (Matthew 5:16).

5 Hindrances to Living by the Word of God

1. Seeking praise from man more than God (John 12:42-43).

2. The tragic traps of tradition (Mark 7:1-13).

3. The hardening of our hearts (Hebrews 4:12-13; Exodus 8:32).

4. Allowing our desires to distort the meaning of Scripture (2 Timothy 4:3-4).

5. The attitude of pride (James 1:21-25).

4 Results of Living by the Word of God

1. A life of dependence on God (Psalm 119:169-176).

2. Depending on God for discernment (vs. 169).

3. Depending on God for deliverance (vs. 170).

4. Depending on God for direction (vs. 176).

10 Reasons Why People Don't Read Their Bibles

1. I don't have time

Remember, we always make time for what's most important to us.

2. I don't know where to start

There's no right or wrong place to start. Try starting at the beginning of any book of the Bible. Or you can follow a Bible reading plan.

3. Reading makes me sleepy

Try switching times and locations. Pace yourself if you need to.

4. The Bible is too confusing

It doesn't have to be! Anything is confusing when you're not familiar with it. Commit to spending a month reading it daily and see how you feel then.

5. I never get anything out of it

If you go to the Bible to "get something," you might consider changing your motivation. Ask God to open your eyes that you might hear from Him. Then put what you read into practice. That's where the reward comes!

6. There are many contradictions in the Bible.

Contradictions are opportunities to study the Scriptures.

7. The Bible is boring

There are challenging parts. Here's a tip: Picture what you're reading, as if it were a movie.

8. I might have to change

You probably will have to change! This is the most difficult aspect of Bible reading. It challenges your beliefs and lifestyle! But the wisdom of God and His love for you assure you that change is good, and that He will help you accomplish that change.

9. *I forget or I get distracted*

If you find your mind wandering, press on. This usually only lasts for a short time. If you can get past a few minutes, your mind will engage.

10. *I'm not smart enough*

God has given us the capability to grasp His Word. We often just lack motivation. If it were your favorite hobby, you would overcome this barrier easily. Stop making excuses, and dive into God's Word!

CHAPTER SIX

Your Praise Is Your Weapon

We are exhorted, challenged, and commanded throughout Scripture to offer praise and worship to the God of all creation. Psalm 150 says, "Praise ye the Lord, praise God in His sanctuary, praise him in the firmament of His power. Praise him for His mighty acts; praise him according to His excellent greatness. Praise him with the sound of the trumpet, praise him with the psaltery and harp. Praise him with the timbrel and dance; praise him with the stringed instruments and organs. Praise him upon the loud cymbals; praise him upon the high sounding cymbals. Let everything that hath breath praise the Lord, praise ye the Lord."

Psalm 149 says, "Praise ye the Lord, sing unto the Lord a new song, and praise him in the congregation of the saints, for the Lord takes pleasure in our praise."

We were created to praise God, and when we do not function in the capacity of our creative purpose, we stand in direct disobedience to God. There are always consequences for those who will not praise Him.

When you neglect to praise God, you forfeit an opportunity to fellowship with Him. Praise is more than some religious ritual performed on a Sunday morning. Authentic praise is the vehicle that ushers you into the divine presence of the almighty God. You probably know the saying, "When the praises go up, the blessings come down," but it should say, "When the praises go up, the *blessor* comes down." Psalm 22:3 says, "God inhabits the praises of His people".

Are You Satisfied with His Presence Alone?

Can you honestly say you want God's presence more than His possessions? God's blessings are inextricably attached to His presence, and that's why the enemy doesn't mind you having things, because you can have things and still be frustrated, depressed, and in bondage. But once you have a real encounter with the divine presence of God, material items won't matter anymore.

Experience the Permanence of Joy

Psalm 16:11 says, "In the presence of the Lord there is fullness of Joy." Joy is a permanent disposition based on contentment. Happiness is a temporary mental resolution based upon your current circumstances. The reason why some believers will not praise Him is because things happening have distracted them, but once you have experienced the joy of the Lord, it no longer matters what happens around you, because God has already released something in you. People can take away your happiness, but they can never take away your joy. Nehemiah said the joy of the Lord was his strength. Even when he was weak, the joy of the Lord gave him the ability to praise God in spite of his sufferings.

When You Give the Enemy an Advantage

Every now and then, someone in my congregation will go missing for a while. When they return, they'll say, "Pastor, the devil has been busy in my life, and I had to take some time to get myself together."

First of all, you can't get yourself together without God. Secondly, when you really learn how to worship, it will change you. No one has entered into the presence of God without experiencing a change in their life. That's why Satan wants you to stay home, depressed and defeated. He knows that one worship experience can tear down every stronghold, shatter every chain, and break every curse in your life. Nothing intimidates the enemy more than a child of God who has been through hell, and wakes up Sunday morning and says, "Devil, I'm still going to church."

In 2 Chronicles 20, King Jehoshaphat of Judah has just received news that the Ammonites, the Moabites, and the Edomites have formed an evil alliance, and they have conspired to attack Judah to destroy the people of God. In verse three, Jehoshaphat "is fearful, but he's prayerful" because he understands that God has a solution to every one of the enemy's advances. In 2 Chronicles 20:14-17, the prophet Jahaziel stands up in the midst of the congregation and says, "King, you don't have to be afraid of the enemies, this battle is not yours but it belongs to God. Tomorrow take your people and go down to the cliff of Ziz, and the Lord is going to be with you." When you understand that God is with you, it doesn't matter who rises up against you.

The next morning, the king assembles his people for battle. In verse 21, the Lord gives them some strange strategies for warfare. He says, "Put the singers, the praisers in front of the army, and let them praise the beauty of holiness." When you march toward the enemy, do not march as an army marching to fight. March as if you are returning from a victory. That's how you can tell when it's the Lord's battle, because He will always assure us of the victory before the fight takes place. God desires you to worship Him before warfare. What an interesting choice of weaponry, worship. Not spears or swords, not arrows or stones. God used praise to bring about their deliverance.

Praise Confuses the Enemy

2 Chronicles 20:22-23 says, "When they began to sing and praise God, he sent an ambush against their enemies, and they ended up destroying each other." Praise God through your struggles and you will confuse the devil greatly. When your loved ones abandon you, when others mistreat you, when you're stabbed in the back, when you're beaten, broken, and abused, don't give Satan the satisfaction of defeating you. Lift your hands in the midst of your storm and cry out "hallelujah" anyhow! If you do, you'll give the devil a nervous breakdown.

Praise Conquers Every Enemy

2 Chronicles 20:24 says, "When Judah came to the place where the enemy was supposed to be, all they saw were dead bodies, and not one enemy escaped." Every one of their enemies (the Ammonites, the Moabites, the Edomites) was destroyed by their praise. The moment they started praising, God started slaying. Let God fight your battles. He can make a clean sweep of every demon you face. Stop wasting your time fighting enemies that He already defeated, and learn how to praise God in advance. The devil's already defeated!

Praise Counteracts the Enemy

The enemy was trying to overtake Judah to destroy the people and seize their goods, but 2 Chronicles 20:25 says, "When Jehoshaphat came to collect the spoil from the battle, there was so much stuff, it took them three days to collect it all." Everything the devil tried to do, God said, "Because you are mine, I'm going to reverse it."

Yes, praise is your weapon!

CHAPTER SEVEN

Good Works

Good works within Christian theology refer to a person's exterior actions. It includes every single thing you do from the time your eyes open in the morning until they close at night. Everything you say and how you say it, to everything you do and how you do it. What you think, what you read, what you watch, and what you desire. Every single thing you do will either be a good work or a bad work in the eyes of God.

Apostle John describes the life of a Christian as walking in the same way in which Jesus walked, which also includes deeds (1 John 2:6). In his letter, Jude describes false teachers as "fruitless trees in late autumn," indicating that true believers should bear fruit in their lives (Jude 12). No matter what a person's actions, salvation comes through faith alone. Ephesians 2:8–9 says, "For by grace ye are saved through faith: and that not of yourselves: it is the gift of God: not of works, lest any man should boast." Salvation is God's gift at God's sole prerogative. Were it achieved by works, men could take pride in their efforts toward holiness, and God's gift of grace would be diminished.

On the other hand, Apostle Paul says that God's chosen one who has been made holy by grace must show faith by actually loving (Galatians 5:6), and in this way obeying the law (i.e. the law or commandment of Christ and His Spirit, see Romans 8:2).

The epistle of James presents a more works-oriented perspective by saying, "Faith without works is dead" (James 2:26). James is not saying that a person is saved by works, but that genuine faith will produce good deeds; however, only faith in Christ saves.

In an article by Dan Corner, he states, "It seems that the only scripture a believer knows about good works is that we are not saved by them (Ephesians 2:8-9)." Sadly, many have adopted an attitude that good works are virtually insignificant. This is flawed theology!

Christians are commanded to let their light shine, which means they are to do good deeds before others, even the unsaved:

- "In the same way, let your light shine before men, that they may see your good deeds and praise your Father in heaven" (Matthew 5:16).

- "Live such good lives among the pagans that, though they accuse you of doing wrong, they may see your good deeds and glorify God on the day he visits us" (1 Peter 2:12).

- The early Christians especially helped Christian widows: "No widow may be put on the list of widows unless she is over sixty, has been faithful to her husband, and is well known for her good deeds, such as bringing up children, showing hospitality, washing the feet of the saints, helping those in trouble and devoting herself to all kinds of good deeds" (1 Timothy 5:9-10).

- Good deeds (and sins) that are not obvious in this life will be revealed on the Judgment Day: "The sins of some men are obvious, reaching the place of judgment ahead of them; the sins of others trail behind them. In the same way, good deeds are obvious, and even those that are not cannot be hidden" (1 Timothy 5:24-25).

- Rich Christians are commanded to be rich in good deeds: "Command those who are rich in this present world not to be arrogant nor to put their hope in wealth, which is so uncertain, but to put their hope in God, who richly provides us with everything for our enjoyment. Command them to do good, to be rich in good deeds, and to be generous and willing to share" (1 Timothy 6:17-18).

- Among other general commands for Christians, we are to consider how we can spur other Christians on towards love and good deeds: "And let us consider how we may spur one another toward love and good deeds (Hebrew 10:24).

- The Christian's life should abound in good deeds: "For we are God's workmanship, created in Christ Jesus to do good works, which God prepared in advance for us to do" (Ephesians 2:10). "And God is able to make all grace abound to you, so that in all things at all times, having all that you need, you will abound in every good work" (2 Corinthians 9:8). "And we pray this in order that you may live a life worthy of the Lord and may please him in every way: bearing fruit in every good work, growing in the knowledge of God," (Colossians 1:10).

- One of our chief Christian aims is to do good works, which can be done if we cleanse ourselves spiritually: "If a man cleanses himself from the latter, he will be an instrument for noble purposes, made holy, useful to the Master and prepared to do any good work" (2 Timothy 2:21).

- Any man of God is completely equipped for every good work with the scriptures alone: "All Scripture is God-breathed and is useful for teaching, rebuking, correcting and training in righteousness, so that the man of God may be thoroughly equipped for every good work" (2 Timothy 3:16-17).

Jesus sacrificed himself to:

1) Redeem a people from all wickedness
2) Purify for himself a people that are His own

Such people are further described as those who are eager to do what is good:

"It [grace] teaches us to say 'no' to ungodliness and worldly passions, and to live self-controlled, upright and godly lives in this present age, while we wait for the blessed hope—the glorious appearing of our great God and Savior, Jesus Christ, who gave himself for us to redeem us from all wickedness and to purify for himself a people that are his very own, eager to do what is good" (Titus 2:12-14).

That word "eager" means zealous. Does that describe you?

Faith Without Good Deeds is Dead

Good deeds must accompany faith. Otherwise, faith is dead.

A specific example of a good deed is giving clothes and food to a fellow Christian who doesn't have such:

- "What good is it, my brothers, if a man claims to have faith but has no deeds? Can such faith save him? Suppose a brother or sister is without clothes and daily food. If one of you says to him, 'Go, I wish you well; keep warm and well fed,' but does nothing about his physical needs, what good is it? In the same way, faith by itself, if it is not accompanied by action, is dead" (James 2:14-17).

James then counters an apparent objection:
"But someone will say, 'You have faith; I have deeds. Show me your faith without deeds, and I will show you my faith by what I do.' You believe that there is one God. Good! Even the demons believe that and shudder. You foolish man, do you want evidence that faith without deeds is useless?" (James 2:18-20).

James goes on to cite the example of Abraham to prove this point. Was not our ancestor Abraham considered righteous for what he did when he offered his son Isaac on the altar? His faith and his actions were working together, and his faith was made complete by what he did. And the scripture was fulfilled that says, "Abraham believed God, and it was credited to him as righteousness." A person is justified by what he does, not by faith alone (James 2:21-24).

Another similar example was Rahab the prostitute:
Rahab the prostitute was considered righteous for what she did when she gave lodging to the spies and sent them off in a different direction. "As the body without the spirit is dead, so faith without deeds is dead (James 2:25-26).

For Rahab to offer protection for the spies was equivalent to risking her life for them. Both Abraham and Rahab are examples of people who had a faith accompanied by good deeds. Their faith was made complete by what they did. Both ends of the moral gamut are shown with Abraham and Rahab.

Paul, the real grace teacher who fought against legalism, taught Christian women the proper way to dress:

- "I also want women to dress modestly, with decency and propriety, not with braided hair or gold or pearls or expensive clothes, but with good deeds, appropriate for women who profess to worship God" (1 Timothy 2:9-10).

For a Christian to receive a great reward, they are told to do good to their enemies:

- "But I tell you who hear me: Love your enemies, do good to those who hate you, bless those who curse you, pray for those who mistreat you. If someone strikes you on one cheek, turn to him the other also. If someone takes your cloak, do not stop him from taking your tunic. Give to everyone who asks you, and if anyone takes what belongs to you, do not demand it back. Do to others as you would have them do to you. If you love those who love you, what credit is that to you? Even 'sinners' love those who love them. And if you do good to those who are good to you, what credit is that to you? Even 'sinners' do that. And if you lend to those from whom you expect repayment, what credit is that to you? Even 'sinners' lend to 'sinners,' expecting to be repaid in full. But love your enemies, do good to them, and lend to them without expecting to get anything back. Then your reward will be great, and you will be sons of the Most High, because he is kind to the ungrateful and wicked" (Luke 6:27-35).

The Lord Jesus concisely described those who actually enter the kingdom of God as those who have done good:

- "Do not be amazed at this, for a time is coming when all who are in their graves will hear his voice and come out, those who have done good will rise to live, and those who have done evil will rise to be condemned" (John 5:28-29).

There are only two paths to pursue: either good or evil:

- "To those who by persistence in doing good seek glory, honor and immortality, he will give eternal life. But for those who are self-seeking and who reject the truth and follow evil, there will be wrath and anger. There will be trouble and distress for every human being who does evil: first for the Jew, then for the Gentile; but glory, honor and peace for everyone who does good: first for the Jew, then for the Gentile" (Rom. 2:7-10).

According to true grace, sowing to please the Spirit, which will result in reaping eternal life, comes down to doing good:

- "The one who sows to please his sinful nature, from that nature will reap destruction; the one who sows to please the Spirit, from the Spirit will reap eternal life. Let us not become weary in doing good, for at the proper time we will reap a harvest if we do not give up. Therefore, as we have opportunity, let us do good to all people, especially to those who belong to the family of believers" (Galatians 6:8-10).

It's possible for any Christian to be prepared to do any good work:

- "Nevertheless, God's solid foundation stands firm, sealed with this inscription: 'The Lord knows those who are his,' and, 'Everyone who confesses the name of the Lord must turn away from wickedness.' In a large house there are articles not only of gold and silver, but also of wood and clay; some are for noble purposes and some for ignoble. If a man cleanses himself from the latter, he will be an instrument for noble purposes, made holy, useful to the Master and prepared to do any good work" (2 Timothy 2:19-21).

Teachers are especially prompted to set an example of doing good:

- "In everything set them an example by doing what is good. In your teaching show integrity, seriousness and soundness of speech that cannot be condemned, so that those who oppose you may be ashamed because they have nothing bad to say about us" (Titus 2:7-8).

First-century Christians were reminded of certain basic truths, including doing whatever is good:

- "Remind the people to be subject to rulers and authorities, to be obedient, to be ready to do whatever is good, to slander no one, to be peaceable and considerate, and to show true humility toward all men" (Titus 3:1-2).

It is profitable for everyone when Christians devote themselves to doing good:

- "This is a trustworthy saying. And I want you to stress these things, so that those who have trusted in God may be careful to devote themselves to doing what is good. These things are excellent and profitable for everyone" (Titus 3:8).

- "Our people must learn to devote themselves to doing what is good, in order that they may provide for daily necessities and not live unproductive lives" (Titus 3:14).

The days of animal sacrifices are over for the Christian, but there are other sacrifices such as doing good:

- "And do not forget to do good and to share with others, for with such sacrifices God is pleased" (Hebrews 13:16).

Many people consider themselves wise and understanding, but are they really? Notice how good deeds play a role in this:

- "Who is wise and understanding among you? Let him show it by his good life, by deeds done in the humility that comes from wisdom (James 3:13).

Good behavior is to be the norm for the Christian, but suffering might be a factor:

- "But in your hearts set apart Christ as Lord. Always be prepared to give an answer to everyone who asks you to give the reason for the hope that you have. But do this with gentleness and respect, keeping a clear conscience, so that those who speak maliciously against your good behavior in Christ may be ashamed of their slander. It is better, if it is God's will, to suffer for doing good than for doing evil" (1 Peter 3:15-17).

Remember, we are not saved by our "works" (Ephesians 2:8-9), but a saving faith in Jesus has plenty of good works with it! Furthermore, a Christian is a slave of righteousness, not a slave of sin anymore!

Most Christians consider themselves definitely saved. When asked why they are so sure, most will tell you how they have spent their whole lives doing good works. They will usually say something like, "I've gone to church just about my whole life, and I have been a pretty good father and husband. I never beat my wife! And if you knew how much I have given to the church and to all those charities. I don't cheat on my income taxes, and I don't break any laws. I have led a good clean Christian life. I'm positive I am going to heaven. I can almost feel the Lord saying to me that I am a cinch to get into heaven. All I ever do is good works."

What they are forgetting is Matthew 7:21. Jesus says, "Not everyone that saith unto me, 'Lord, Lord', shall enter into the kingdom of heaven; but he that doeth the will of the Father which is in heaven."

The will of the Father? Doesn't that mean doing all kinds of good charitable works and helping people? Isn't that the will of the Father? Being a good person and living a good clean life? Aren't those the things that will get you into heaven?

Look at what the Word of God tells us:

Romans 4:2 says, "If Abraham was justified by works, then he has something to boast about, but not before God."

There are many verses in the Bible that tell us that our good works alone will do absolutely nothing to gain us eternal life. Isaiah 64:6 says, "But we are all like an unclean thing, and all our righteous deeds are like filthy rags."

To give you an idea of how absurd the idea of working your way into heaven by doing good works is, consider this. Can you just imagine standing before the gates of heaven with a bucket full of filthy rags, and telling God you are ready to come in, and that you have a whole bunch of nice filthy rags that you want to use as payment for your entrance fee into heaven?

If you base your salvation and your entrance into heaven on your "good works", then you are looking inward for your salvation. Your hope for heaven is based upon the fact that you are a pretty good person, that you have helped other people, that you have given your money, that you have followed the golden rule. In other words you have saved you. Glory be to you.

It kind of makes you wonder why you even need God. Faith in Christ is of little importance. If a person can earn forgiveness of sins and everlasting life through one's own efforts, then why was Jesus Christ even born? What was the purpose of His suffering and His horrible death? Why did He have to shed His blood and rise from the dead? What was the reason for His victories over sin, death, and the devil? If men can overcome these evils by their own endeavor, why did God (in the form of Jesus Christ) even have to come down to earth?

Tongues cannot express, nor hearts conceive, what a terrible thing it is to make Christ worthless.

Many people also believe that salvation is obtained by a combination of faith in Christ and good works. However, that says that it takes you and God to save you. If that is the case, then we can no longer say, "Glory be to God." Instead we should say, "Glory be to us." The Bible says God will not share His glory with another. The only way to attain salvation is by having complete faith in Jesus Christ.

- We are saved by Christ.

- Through faith

Galatians 2:16 says, "Knowing that a man is not justified by the works of the law, but by faith in Jesus Christ."

One of the clearest teachings in the entire Bible is that we are saved through grace by faith in Jesus Christ only. Not by our own personal worthiness. Paul said, "It is a gift of God, not of works, lest any man should boast." We forget that the only way into heaven is by the grace of God and not by "good works." In fact, many good works are done only to impress others. The following verses are good examples of this:

- (John 12:43): "They loved the praise of men more than the praise of God."

- (Matthew 5:8-9): "These people draw near to me with their mouth, and honor me with their lips, but their heart is far from me. And in vain they worship me, teaching as doctrines the commandments of men."

That leaves us with the question: Well, what about good works? Don't they matter? Aren't they important? Once you have been saved, you quickly find that true faith cannot be idle. Once we are saved we are suddenly energized by the Holy Spirit. We now discover that we have Jesus Christ living within us. And when He saved us, He did something really remarkable. He performed a surgery on us. He proceeded to rip out our old vile, dirty, filthy, repulsive, evil-filled hearts. And in its place, He put a brand new radiant and brilliant heart, filled with goodness and love and light.

Ezekiel 36:26 says, "A new heart I will give you, and a new spirit I will put within you; and I will remove from your body the heart of stone and give you a heart of flesh."

By "heart" I do not mean that cardiac muscle that lies inside your chest and keeps your physical body alive. When the term "heart" is used in the Bible, it usually is referring to the very core of a person. The heart of a person is the person's character, his integrity.

Matthew 5:8 says, "Blessed are the pure in heart, since they will see God." The Lord is referring to the person who has a character that He approves of, a character that is pleasing to Him, that He is proud of, a character completely given over to Jesus Christ.

The Secret Behind Good Works

Good works will never ever get you saved! You can do good works from sun up until sundown and they will not get you one step closer to heaven. In fact, you could live 10 million years and do 10 million good deeds every single day, and all of those deeds combined would not get you one inch closer to salvation and eternal life. You cannot behave yourself into heaven.

You are saved by one thing and one thing only: by having complete faith in Jesus Christ. In order to receive salvation, you must truly believe that Jesus Christ is the son of God, and that He left heaven and came to earth to die on the cross at Calvary, and that the blood that He shed on that cross allowed you to have your sins forgiven. You must repent of your sins and you must ask God to forgive you of those sins. If you can do those few simple things, and at the same time accept the death of Jesus Christ as full payment for all of your sins both past, present, and future, then you will be born again and you will have eternal salvation.

The most important thing for the believer is to become righteous in the eyes of God. To do that, Jesus Christ must live inside you. Righteousness means you have surrendered your life to Jesus Christ, and that you follow Him, not the world.

You are righteous by faith, not by works. But once you're saved, you will have a tremendous desire to serve Christ and do good works. Faith is invisible. You cannot judge a person's faith by his words because humans lie. But you can see the results of faith by the life we live, by the way we react on a daily basis to the various circumstances that come our way. Faith without works is like a car without wheels.

If you see an elderly lady waiting to cross a busy street, and you take her arm, and patiently help her across the street, that would be considered a "good work." However, if you shove her aside and tell her that she is just slowing you down, then I'm sure you would consider that a "bad work." Likewise, every single action you perform can be considered either a good work or a bad work in the eyes of God. Colossians 1:21 says, "Indeed, you were once alienated and enemies because your minds were on works that were wicked."

Faith and good works do go together, but you must first have faith in order for the good works to matter. James says, "And I shall show you my faith by my works" (James 2:18).

The steps of faith and good works can be seen like this.

- You are saved.

- You now have faith in Jesus Christ whom you now want to please.

- This faith leaves you with a desire to do good works.

- Good works causes your faith to grow even more.

- More faith spurs you to do even more good works.

- Through faith, you continually desire to obey Jesus Christ.

James 2:22 says, "By his works is his faith perfected." James 2:26 says, "Faith without works is dead."

What Do Good Works Really Mean?

There is a lot more to good works than helping a lady across the street. First, it means loving God and trusting Him completely. It also means obeying the 10 commandments of God. It means that when you sin, you ask for forgiveness and make a real effort to avoid that sin again. It means prayer to God and the reading of His Word. It also means loving your fellow man and helping him whenever you get a chance. It means forgiving people when they wrong you. It means not taking advantage of another person, but instead hoping for the best for them. It means not getting angry or seeking revenge toward another person. It means thinking good thoughts instead of evil thoughts.

So what are good works? It means allowing Jesus Christ to guide you step-by-step through each and every day of your life. When you allow God to work through you, then you are allowing God to carry out His plan, to do His work, to do His will, all for His own purposes and His own reasons, and all done through you.

James 2:14-18 says, "My brothers and sisters, if people say they have faith, but do nothing, their faith is worth nothing. Can faith like that save them? A brother or sister in Christ might need clothes or food. But if you say to that person, 'God be with you! I do hope you stay warm and get plenty to eat,' but you do not give what that person needs, then your words are hollow and worth nothing. In the same way, faith that is alone—that does nothing—is dead. Someone might say, 'You have faith, but I have deeds. Show me your faith without doing anything, and I will show you my faith by what I do'" (New Century Version).

James makes the point that someone who says he has faith yet does not spend his life doing "good works" is deceiving themselves. Why? Because if he was truly saved and had the Holy Spirit and Jesus Christ dwelling within him, he would want to spend the rest of his life doing nothing but good works.

Helping those in need will not earn you salvation, but those who have salvation will go out of their way to help those in need. Keeping the laws and commandments of God will not gain you salvation, but those who have salvation will have a powerful inner desire to keep and obey all of his laws.

Reading the Word of God will not obtain for you salvation, but those who are saved will have a tremendous urge to read and study the Word of God. Those moments spent in prayer and praise to God will not obtain for you eternal life and eternal salvation, but true believers will have hearts that want to pray and praise God constantly.

Matthew 5:16 says, "Let your light shine before men, so that they may see your good works and glorify your Father who is in heaven."

Those who have salvation will show it through all the things they do, each and every day of their lives. So if you really think about it, it *is* our actions and deeds that reflect what we really believe in. And that is why our actions are so extremely important to God. For it is our actions that tell God whether we have Jesus Christ living within our hearts. Our actions and deeds tell God whether we are a Christ hater or a Christ lover.

2 Corinthians 5:10 says, "For all of us must appear before Christ, to be judged by him. We will each receive what we deserve, according to everything we have done, good or bad, while in the body."

Matthew 16:24 says, "For the Son of Man is going to come in his Father's glory with his angels, and then he will reward each person according to what he has done."

Ephesians 2:10 says, "For we are His workmanship, created in Christ Jesus, for good works, which God prepared beforehand that we should walk in them."

Revelation 22:12 says, "And behold, I am coming quickly, and my reward is with me, to give to every one according to his work."

Ecclesiastes 12:14 says, "For God will bring every work into judgment, including every hidden thing, whether good or evil."

Most Christians think that good works means giving money or time to charities. But in reality that is only an extremely small part. There is a whole world of good works out there because every single thing we do in our lives can be considered a work.

Eternal salvation starts with faith but other things soon follow (2 Peter 1:5-8):

- Supply to your faith virtue.

- And to virtue supply knowledge.

- And to knowledge supply self-control.

- And to self-control supply endurance.

- And to endurance supply godly devotion.

- And to godly devotion supply brotherly affection.

- And to brotherly affection supply love.

- So you are kept from being ineffective or unfruitful in the knowledge of our Lord Jesus Christ.

God is not looking for those who merely speak the words of Christ. He wants those who live the words of Christ.

When a person dies and their soul steps through that curtain to be with the Lord, they take absolutely nothing with them except for one thing: the accumulation of a lifetime of works. It is spelled out so very clearly in Revelation 14:13, Revelation 19:8, and in Revelation 20:12.

- Revelation 14:13: "And I heard a voice out of heaven say: Write, happy are the dead who die in union with the Lord from this time onward. Yes, says the Spirit, let them rest from their labors for the things they do go right with them."

- Revelation 19:8: "It was granted her to be clothed with fine linen, bright and pure, for the fine linen is the righteous deeds of the saints."

- Revelation 20:12: "And I saw the dead, the great and the small, standing before the throne; and books were opened: and another book was opened, which is the book of life: and the dead were judged out of the things which were written in the books, according to their works."

And finally, in almost the very last thing He told us in the Bible, the Lord spoke of good works and their extreme importance. In Revelation 22:12 the Lord tells us, "And behold, I am coming quickly, and My reward is with Me, to give to everyone according to his work."

CHAPTER EIGHT

The Consequences Of Not Spending Time With God

Hear me, you heavens! Listen, earth! For the Lord has spoken: "I reared children and brought them up, but they have rebelled against me. The ox knows its master, the donkey its owner's manger, but Israel does not know, my people do not understand." Woe to the sinful nation, a people whose guilt is great, a brood of evildoers, children given to corruption! They have forsaken the Lord; they have spurned the Holy One of Israel and turned their backs on him. — **Isaiah 1:2-4**

God's greatest desire for His people is to dwell with them in blissful harmony in a relationship. There is nothing that your Heavenly Father wants more than to spend quality time with His prized creation, man. Unfortunately, there are many Christians who have no desire at all to fellowship with God, and as a consequence they fail to enjoy life as their Creator intended.

What Makes A Christian Not Want To Spend Time With God?

1. When we are blinded by our own successes.

2. When we are influenced by the corruptness of this world.

3. When God is not our priority anymore.

4. When we give up on the struggle to live right.

5. When sin dominates our lives.

There Are Certain Needs Which Are not Being Met

But my God shall supply all your need according to his riches in glory by Christ Jesus. — **Philippians 4:19**

a. The need for love (John 3:16)

b. The need for companionship (Hebrews 15:5)

c. The need for security (John 10:28)

You Become Exposed to the Agenda of the Enemy

The thief cometh not, but for to steal, and to kill, and to destroy: I am come that they might have life, and that they might have it more abundantly. — **John 10:10**

a. To steal (What specifically has Satan stolen from you?).

b. To kill (dead momentum, dead dreams, dead people).

c. To destroy (everything that is right).

CHAPTER NINE

Here I Am To Worship

Now when Jesus was born in Bethlehem of Judaea in the days of Herod the king, behold, there came wise men from the east to Jerusalem, Saying, Where is he that is born King of the Jews? For we have seen his star in the east, and are come to worship him. When Herod the king had heard these things, he was troubled, and all Jerusalem with him. And when he had gathered all the chief priests and scribes of the people together, he demanded of them where Christ should be born. And they said unto him, In Bethlehem of Judaea: for thus it is written by the prophet, and thou Bethlehem, in the land of Juda, art not the least among the princes of Juda: for out of thee shall come a Governor, that shall rule my people Israel. Then Herod, when he had privily called the wise men, enquired of them diligently what time the star appeared. And he sent them to Bethlehem, and said, Go and search diligently for the young child; and when ye have found him, bring me word again, that I may come and worship him also. When they had heard the king, they departed; and, lo, the star, which they saw in the east, went before them, till it came and stood over where the young child was. When they saw the star, they rejoiced with exceeding great joy. And when they were come into the house, they saw the young child with Mary his mother, and fell down, and worshipped him: and when they had opened their treasures, they presented unto him gifts; gold, and frankincense and myrrh. And being warned of God in a

> *dream that they should not return to Herod, they departed into their own country another way.* — **Matthew 2:1-12**

One of the things that sets our church apart from many other churches is our attitude and approach to worship. Most of the first-time visitors inevitably say the same thing. They may not remember the title of the sermon; they may not remember the words to the songs; they may not even remember the name of the church, but what they do remember is how they felt in the midst of life-changing, liberating worship. We have people in our church who are seriously committed to worshipping God. Every time they come into the sanctuary, they view it as an opportunity, not just an obligation to enter into the presence of Yahweh. They don't need to be primed in order to worship. As soon as the service begins, their hearts are ready and eager to experience God.

An atmosphere of authentic worship will change your life. How many times have you come to church burdened with problems and dilemmas, and something happens in the worship that changes your perspective about your situation? That's why the devil will try everything to prevent you from coming to church, because he knows there is power in your praise. Where the Spirit of the Lord is, there is liberty.

Worship destroys the yoke of bondage, heals the broken heart, strengthens your faith in God, encourages your soul, eliminates fear, and puts things back in their proper perspective. There is only one question that needs to be settled about God. The question is: *Is He worthy?* If you really believe our God is worthy of all honor, praise, and glory, your immediate response will be to worship Him.

The word worship is a combination of two words, "worth and ship." It implies to send worth to a particular person. When you ascribe worship to God, you are implying that He is worth being the object of your worship. That's why you can lift your hands even when you're not feeling your best, because He's worth it. Don't get it twisted. Performance does not define God. He is not worthy based on what He does, but He is worthy because of who He is. He is God!

When we worship God in spirit and in truth, 3 things will happen:

1. There Is an Inhabitation

But thou art holy, O thou that inhabitest the praises of Israel. — **Psalm 22:3**

God inhabits the praise of His people. To inhabit means to dwell, to sit or to occupy. When we worship God, He shows up as a King to be enthroned. Where there is true worship, you can rest assured God is going to show up. His presence must become the priority of your praise, not just His blessings in your life, because in His presence there is fullness. Everything you will ever need is inextricably tied to His presence. Believe it or not, you need His presence more than you need healing, more than you need a financial breakthrough, more than you need a man or woman in your life, more than you need reliable transportation, because in His presence there is fullness.

2. There Is Revelation

In Isaiah 6:1-9, Isaiah worships, and in the midst of his worship, God reveals three things to him:

First Revelation: *How Isaiah Saw God*

Isaiah 6:1 says, "I saw him high and lifted up, and His train filled the temple." God is exalted!

Second Revelation: *How Isaiah Saw Himself*

Isaiah 6:5 says, "Woe is me, for I am undone! Because I am a man of unclean lips." Once Isaiah recognized the perfect presence of God, he was then able to see his own imperfections. When you stand next to other people and compare yourself to their presence, you look pretty good, but when you compare yourself to the holy presence of God, we are all undone in one way or another.

Third Revelation: *How Isaiah Saw Others*

Isaiah 6:5 says, "I dwell in the midst of a people of unclean lips; for my eyes have seen the King, the Lord of hosts." Isaiah realized he wasn't the only one who was undone. He realized there were people all around him that needed God's perfect presence.

You Become What You Worship

We as human beings have the tendency to emulate what we admire by becoming what we worship. That's why God detests idolatry, because when we worship idols, we begin to take on the character and nature of them. Psalm 115:4-8 says, "But their idols are silver and gold, made by human hands. They have mouths, but cannot speak, eyes, but cannot see. They have ears, but cannot hear, noses, but cannot smell. They have hands, but cannot feel, feet, but cannot walk, nor can they utter a sound with their throats. Those who make them will be like them, and so will all who trust in them."

Whatever and whoever you worship, you will become. If you worship money, you will become a greedy person. If you worship power, you will become corrupt. If you worship sex, you will become lustful. But when you worship Jesus, you will become like Christ!

The Wise Men and How They Worshipped

In Matthew 2, the wise men from the East (Persia) traveled a great distance to pay homage to baby Jesus, the newborn King. The wise men had a clear purpose for traveling so far. They came to worship Jesus. They were educated men, dedicated to the study of science, magic and astrology. For months, they followed the star that signaled the birth of the Messiah. By the time they arrived, Jesus was not in a manger, but rather in a house with His parents. And when they saw the Child, they immediately began to worship Him. These wise men provide a sterling example of true worship.

4 Principles the Wise Men Teach Us About True Worship

1) True Worship Centers Around God

Matthew 2:2 says, "Where is He that is born King of the Jews? For we have seen His star in the East and have come to worship Him." The wise men are not there on a sightseeing expedition. They're not there to evaluate Joseph or congratulate Mary. The sole purpose for coming into the house is to worship Jesus. Which brings me to a question. What is your purpose for entering God's house? Did you come to sightsee or evaluate? Are you here to glorify others or to glorify God?

Golden Words

Gabby Douglas started out life homeless. Her family lived in the back of a van for nearly a year after she was born. Soon after, they were taken in by relatives. Then, her father abandoned them, leaving her mother to support four young children on her own. One of the few African Americans in her gymnastics class, Douglas claimed she was cruelly taunted by her former coach and teammates at Excalibur Gym, who told her to get a nose job and sometimes described her as their slave. Months before the London Olympics, she thought about quitting gymnastics for a fast-food job. She went on to become the first African American female to win gold in Olympic history. After receiving her medal, the very first words out of her mouth were, "All glory goes to God!"

2) True Worship Involves Your Whole Being

Matthew 2:11 says, "When coming into the house, they saw the child with His mother Mary, and they bowed down and worshipped him." This gesture is both a sign of reverence and respect. When we worship God authentically, we must learn to prostrate ourselves before the presence of God. Sometimes you have to lie on your face to give God the glory He deserves.

Lower Yourself To See God's Beauty

A man was walking through an art gallery when he came upon a picture of the Lord Jesus dying upon the cross. He stopped and looked at the beautiful portrait of Christ's love. As he stared into the face of Christ, so full of agony, the gallery guard tapped him on the shoulder. "Lower," the guard said. "The artist painted this picture to be appreciated from a lower position." So the man bent down. From this lower position, he observed new beauties in the picture not previously shown. "Lower still," said the guard. So the man knelt down on one knee and looked up into the face of Christ. The new vantage point yielded new beauties to behold. But motioning with his torch toward the ground, the guard said, "Lower. You've got to go lower."

The man now dropped down to two knees and looked up. Only then as he looked up at the painting from such a low posture could he realize the artist's intended perspective. Only then could he see the full beauty of the cross. Is the same not true in worship? Only as we position ourselves lower and lower in humble submission can we behold more fully the glories of our wonderful Lord.

3) True Worship Includes Our Offering

Matthew 2:11 says, "They opened their treasures and presented him with gifts of gold, of incense and of myrrh." The reason we give monetary offerings to God is not because He lacks money. Our Almighty God, being entirely self-sufficient, requires no gift from frail humanity to sustain him in any way.

Psalm 50:9-12 says, "I have no need of a bull from your stall, or goats from your pens, for every animal of the forest is mine, and the cattle on a thousand hills. If I were hungry I would not tell you, for the world is mine and all that is within it." Then why do we give to God? Our monetary gifts are tokens to express our gratitude to God for what He has given us. Giving is the tangible way to show our hearts to God. Our monetary gift is an indicator of our love for God.

Jesus said in Matthew 6:21, "Where you treasure is, there your heart will be also." Maybe you're thinking, "Just because I don't give, doesn't mean I don't love God!" Tell that to your spouse. No one wants to only hear that you love them and never be shown.

One African proverb says that you can give without loving, but you cannot love without giving. By presenting Jesus with expensive gifts, the wise men demonstrated their sincerity in paying homage to Jesus.

4) *True Worship Requires Our Obedience*

Matthew 2:12 says, "Having been warned in a dream by an angel not to go back to Herod, they returned to their country by another route." The real test of our hearts is not how we worship or how much money we give, but how much we obey His Word in our daily lives. True worship is not just lip service or outward performance, but our obedience to God. Obedience is better than sacrifice.

To Obey Is Better Than Sacrifice

Elisabeth Elliot tells the story of when she and her brother, Tom, were small children. Their mother would let Tom play with paper bags that she had saved as long as he put them away afterwards. One day she walked into the kitchen to find them strewn all over the floor. Tom was in another room at the piano with his father singing hymns.

When their mother called him to the kitchen to tidy up the paper bags, he protested, "But Mum, I want to sing Jesus loves me this I know." His father said, "It's no good singing God's praise if you're disobedient. To obey is better than sacrifice."

Stand Your Ground

1 Corinthians 15:58 says, "Therefore my beloved brethren, be ye steadfast, unmovable, always abounding in the work of the Lord, for as much as you know that your labor is not in vain in the Lord."

In the fall of 2005, the state of Florida passed into law "self-defense legislation" known as, "Stand Your Ground." Essentially, the Stand Your Ground laws are a revocation of the duty to retreat; that under certain circumstances, individuals who perceive themselves to be victims of a potential violent act can use deadly force to defend themselves without first attempting to retreat from the danger. We are living in a time when we need to implement some Stand Your Ground laws in the church of Jesus Christ.

We as Christians need to take a stand for righteousness and defend our faith against the corruption of sin. As a society, we've become too tolerant of sin and wickedness. It seems like anything goes now, and if you raise your voice to speak against immorality or ungodliness, you are viewed as a bad person or a hater.

We have allowed the world to redefine Christianity. Now it's nothing more than a religion of convenient love with no regard to the laws and commands of Jesus Christ. We want to be accepted, but we don't want to change. All the while, the sanctity of marriage is under attack, the fabric of the family is being torn apart, wickedness is parading itself through the church, we've exchanged holiness for a hallelujah, and we don't preach and teach sanctification but rather satisfaction.

Are you sick and tired of being bullied by the ways of this world? Are you ready to take a stand and say, "I don't care who gets mad. The wages of sin is still death and the gift of God is eternal life!"

Hebrews 12:1 says, "Work at living in peace with everyone, and work at living a holy life, for those who are not holy will not see the Lord." When the body of Christ is silent about sin and when the church won't stand her ground against ungodliness, we give room for satanic activity in the company of believers, and we miss the opportunity to witness for our God in the company of sinners.

3 Reasons Why Christians Won't Stand Their Ground

1) We Don't Want To Be Persecuted

If you're a believer, the devil has already plastered up a wanted poster in hell with your picture on it. Any time you raise a flag for God, you will be targeted by the enemy as a threat. People will label you, turn on you, lie to you. Every now and then your relationship with Christ will get you into some trouble. If it hasn't gotten you in to any trouble yet, it may be because nobody can tell which side you're on.

Ever heard of the name Joseph of Arimathea in Scripture? He was a member of the Sanhedrin Counsel, a group of seventy men comprised of elders, scribes and high priests. John 19:38 says, "Joseph of Arimathea is a secret disciple of Jesus Christ." He doesn't want anyone to know he follows Jesus, because he doesn't want to suffer or be persecuted. But here lies the paradox: You are in secret because you don't want to suffer, but you're suffering because you are in secret.

2) We May Have To Stand Alone

When you take a stand for the things of God, it's not going to be popular. There will be times when you'll need to stand your ground without the support of your family and friends. During those times, you must take confidence in this fact: that God will never allow you to take a stand for Him without Him standing right alongside you in power and strength. You don't need a crowd of people in order to make a decision for Christ. All you need is the assurance that the Lord is with you!

In Daniel 6, Daniel's coworkers became jealous of him, so they concocted a devilish plot for King Darius to make a decree that stated if anyone prayed or petitioned to any other god or man, other than King Darius, for the next thirty days, they would be cast into the den of lions. When Daniel found out about the decree, he went into his house and prayed three times a day, giving thanks to God. When they threw Daniel into the lion's den, the lions did not harm him, because God sent angels to keep him safe. Remember, the power you have in Christ is both invisible and invincible. That type of power doesn't require a bunch of people. Sometimes it's just you and God keeping things afloat, taking care of your children, paying bills, keeping the peace at home, and so on. But that's okay. God is more than enough.

3) We Don't Feel That It's Worth It

In 1 Corinthians 15, the Apostle Paul emphasizes that our labor is not in vain. You may not see the results from your efforts. It may seem like it's not making a difference right now, but God is using your experience for a greater impact. You're not going through what you are going through for nothing. God is up to something that has eternal implications. It's worth it! 1 Corinthians 15 is the doctrine concerning the resurrection of Jesus Christ and the resurrection of the saints, those who die for the Lord. Paul writes to inspire and to a discouraged and despondent church, that even in the midst of severe persecution and hardship, they can look to the resurrection of Jesus and find hope for the future.

It doesn't matter how big your problem is. As long as it's not bigger than a dead Jesus, God can handle your situation. And because Jesus Christ rose from the dead and conquered death, we who are followers will experience that same resurrection at His second coming.

1 Corinthians 15:51-54 says, "Behold I show you a mystery, we shall not all sleep, but we shall all be changed. In a moment, in the twinkling of an eye, when the trumpet sounds, the dead in Christ shall rise, and this corruptible body must put on incorruption, and death shall be swallowed up in victory."

Paul concludes 1 Corinthians 15 by telling the saints at Corinth to do three things: 1) Be steadfast 2) Be unmovable and 3) always do the work of the Lord.

Be Steadfast: Progress in the Right Direction

The word steadfast means to be steady, fixed, consistent, and focused in your walk with God. Stay on the right path and don't allow yourself to get distracted or detached from your faith. Keep moving onward and forward in your Christian journey. You've come too far to give up now. You are closer now to the thing that God promised you than ever before. Your destiny is within your reach. If you stumble, that's okay. If you fall, get back up. If you get tired, ask God to give you strength. If you get lonely, ask the Lord to take you by the hand. If you feel like you can't take another step, take another step. Don't let anybody turn you from the faith.

Be Unmovable: Stay Planted in the Right Doctrine

The word unmovable means to be unshakeable and unbreakable. It doesn't mean brittle or unbendable, but it does mean to be firmly established in a place or position. Don't let anybody pull you away from what you believe concerning the gospel of Jesus Christ. Don't believe every parking lot prophecy spoken over your life. Stand for what you know to be true according to the gospel of Jesus Christ. Any doctrine that denies the truth of the resurrection of Christ is not sound doctrine at all. That's why we are exhorted throughout scripture to study the Word of God.

In 2 Timothy 4 it says, "There will come a time when people will not want to hear sound doctrine, but they shall turn away their ears from the truth, to fables." Fables are stories and tales and allegories that may or may not be true. We say a lot of things in our vernacular that sounds biblical but cannot be found in Scripture. When you don't have doctrine then you are subject to believe anything and everybody! You need an anchor that can hold you when the storms of life rage all around you.

Consistently Practice the Right Disciplines

"Be always abounding in the work of the Lord" (1 Corinthians 15:58).

CHAPTER TEN

Share Jesus Now

A witness is someone who attests to a fact. In order to be an effective witness for Christ, one must have firsthand knowledge of Him. If you have experienced new life in Jesus Christ, you have the responsibility and privilege to give an account of His love and forgiveness, both verbally and in the way you live your life. This is witnessing!

6 Conditions of a Successful Witness

1. Having your own personal experience of salvation (John 15:4-5).

2. Living lives that are exemplary (2 Timothy 2:21).

3. Possessing a working knowledge of the Word (2 Timothy 2:15).

4. Committed to a life of prayer (Matthew 21:22).

5. A genuine love for souls (Romans 10:1).

6. Perseverance (Galatians 6:9).

The Theme of Our Witness is Jesus Christ

(See 1 Corinthians 15:1-4, Romans 10:9-10, 1 Corinthians 2:2, John 14:6, John 3:16)

- The gospel is the death, burial and resurrection of Jesus Christ.

- The gospel explains the sacrifice of Christ.

- The gospel expresses the love of God.

The Power of Our Witness is the Holy Spirit

(See Matthew 5:16, Titus 3:5, Acts 1:8)

- The Holy Spirit equips us to witness.

- The Holy Spirit transforms lives.

- The Holy Spirit enables us to let our lights shine.

The Validity of our Witness is Holy Living

(See Philippians 2:15, Galatians 5:22, John 15:1-8)

- Blamelessness should be our goal.

- Bearing fruit should be our goal.

And so I leave you with perhaps the most important fill-in-the-blank you've ever encountered, and I challenge you to complete the following statement using your own words:

"Because Christ died for my sins, and rose from the dead, He now lives within me, therefore I _____."

About The Author

Pastor James W. Thomas is the Founder and Senior Pastor of The Rhema Life Fellowship Church in Plano, Texas. With a passion to see the body of Christ engaged in a fruitful and meaningful relationship with the Creator, Pastor Thomas encourages Christians of all ages to commit to spending quality time with God each day. Pastor Thomas (JT), is a multi-gifted international motivational speaker and teacher, and has earned degrees from The Covington Theological Seminary in Georgia.

Phone: 1-469-467-7575
Web: www.rhemachurchplano.com
Email: rhemalife@sbcglobal.net

About SermonToBook.Com

SermonToBook.com began with a simple belief: that sermons should be touching lives, *not* collecting dust. That's why we turn sermons into high-quality books that are accessible to people all over the globe.

Turning your sermon or sermon series into a book exposes more people to God's Word, better equips you for counseling, accelerates future sermon prep, adds credibility to your ministry, and even helps make ends meet during tight times.

John 21:25 tells us that the world itself couldn't contain the books that would be written about the work of Jesus Christ. Our mission is to try anyway. Because, in Heaven, there will no longer be a need for sermons or books. Our time is now.

If God so leads you, we'd love to work with you on your sermon or sermon series.

Visit www.sermontobook.com to learn more.

YOUR PROBLEMS HAVE PURPOSE

Understanding God's Plan for Your Life

Steve Bozeman